MW00900149

THIS COLORING BOOK BELONGS TO:

YOU MUST BE
MISTAKING ME
FOR A
NURSING
STUDENT
WHO GIVES A
SHIT!

NEVER
UNDERESTIMATE A
NURSING
STUDENT
WHO SURVIVED THE
PANDEMIC

I'M NOT
RESPONSIBLE
FOR WHAT
MY FACE
DOES WHEN YOU
TALK

I HATE BEING
Sexy
BUT I'M A
NURSING
STUDENT
SO I CAN'T HELP

World's
Okayest
Nursing
Student

I'VE 99
PROBLEMS
BUT
COLORING
AIN'T ONE

I'M A
NURSING STUDENT
WHAT'S YOUR
SUPER
POWER?

Sorry
I'M DONE
HELPING
ASSHOLES
Today

THIS
Nursing
Student
IS OFF
DUTY

Three horrible facts:
1- Today is not Friday.
2- Tomorrow is not Friday.
3- Even the day after tomorrow is not Friday.

STFU!
JUST ASSUME
I'M ALWAYS
RIGHT

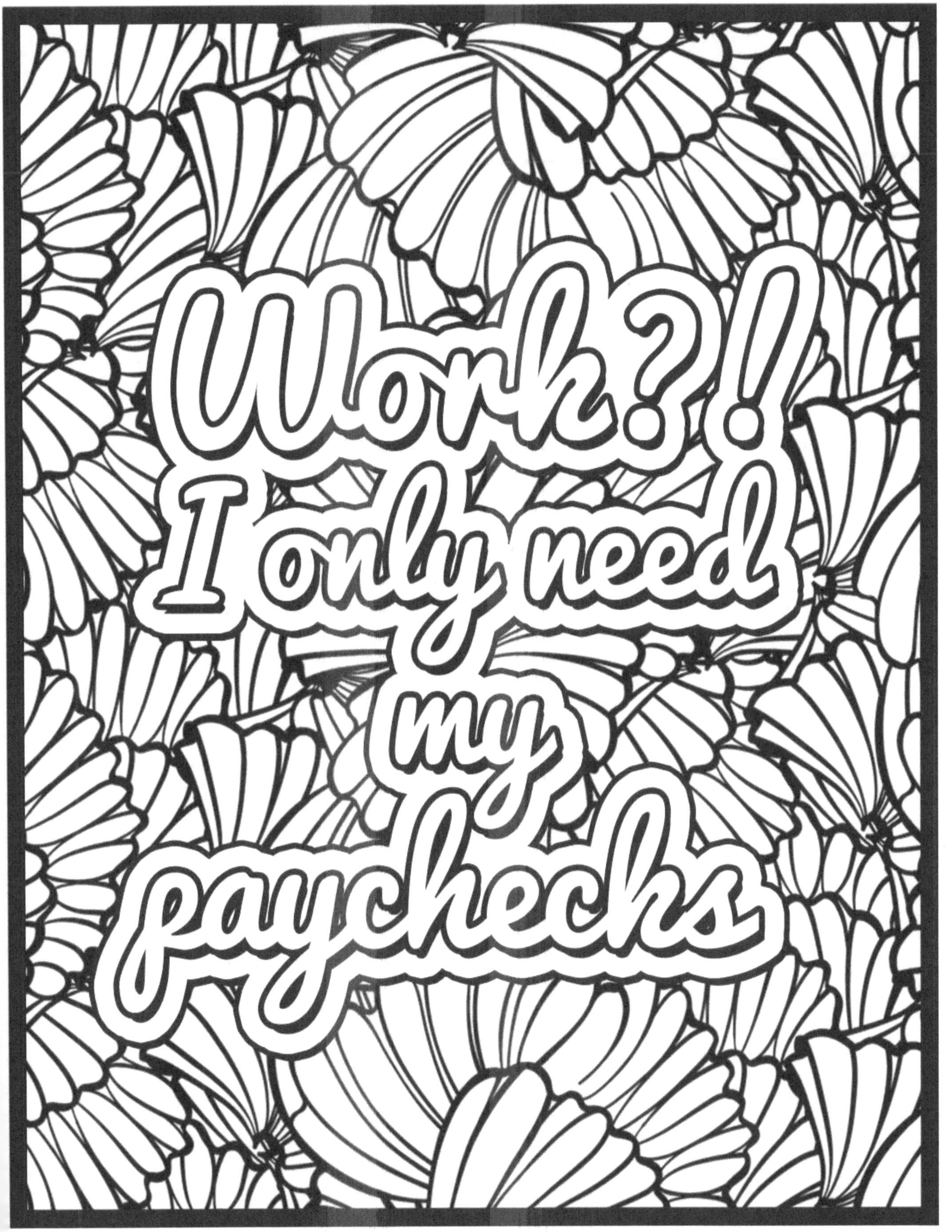
Work?!
I only need
my
paychecks

THIS
NURSING
STUDENT
NEEDS A
MOTHER
FUCKING
DRINK

SOME PEOPLE
JUST NEED A
High-Five
(IN THE FACE)

NURSING
STUDENT
LLAMA
AIN'T GOT
TIME FOR
YOUR DRAMA

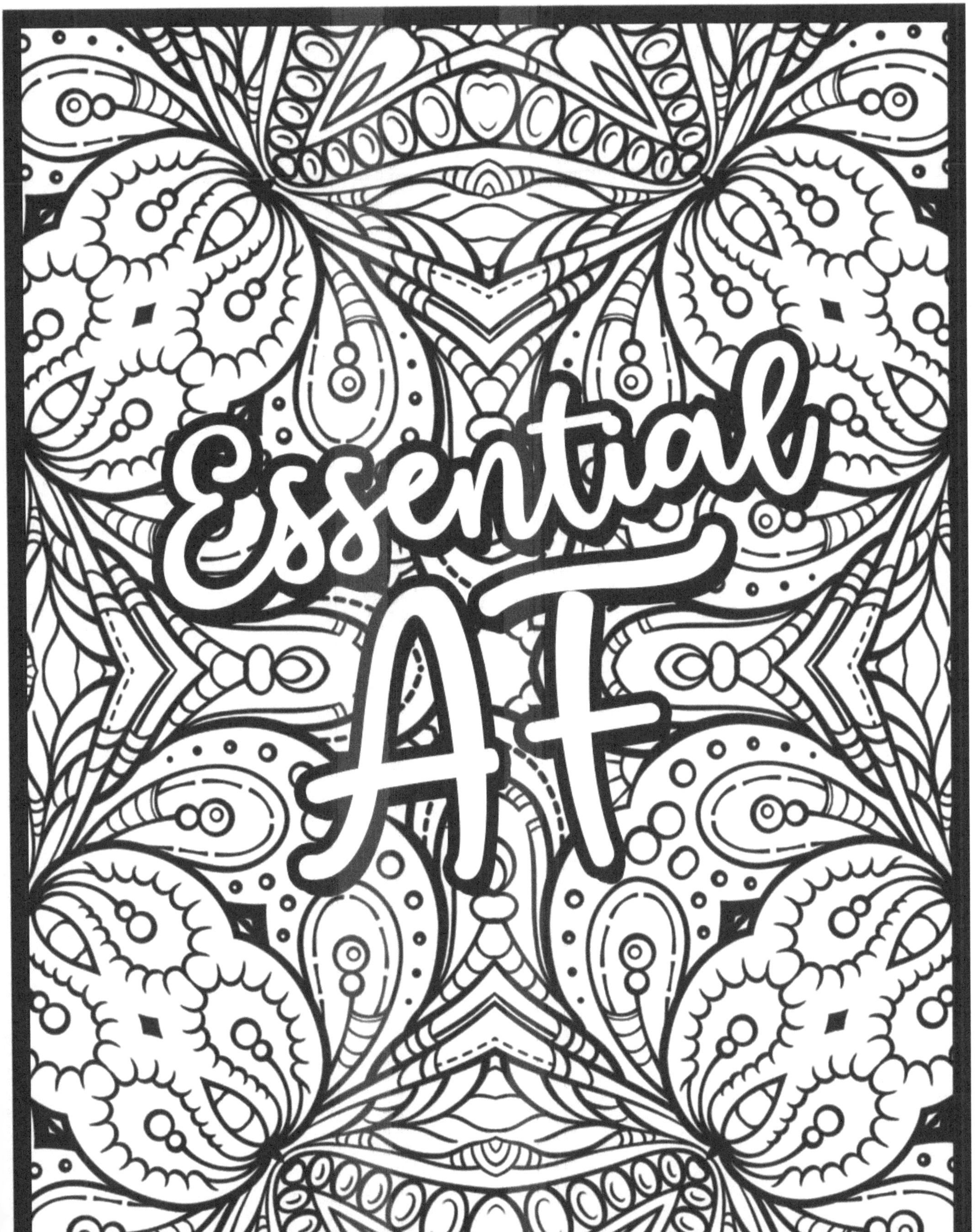
Essential
AF

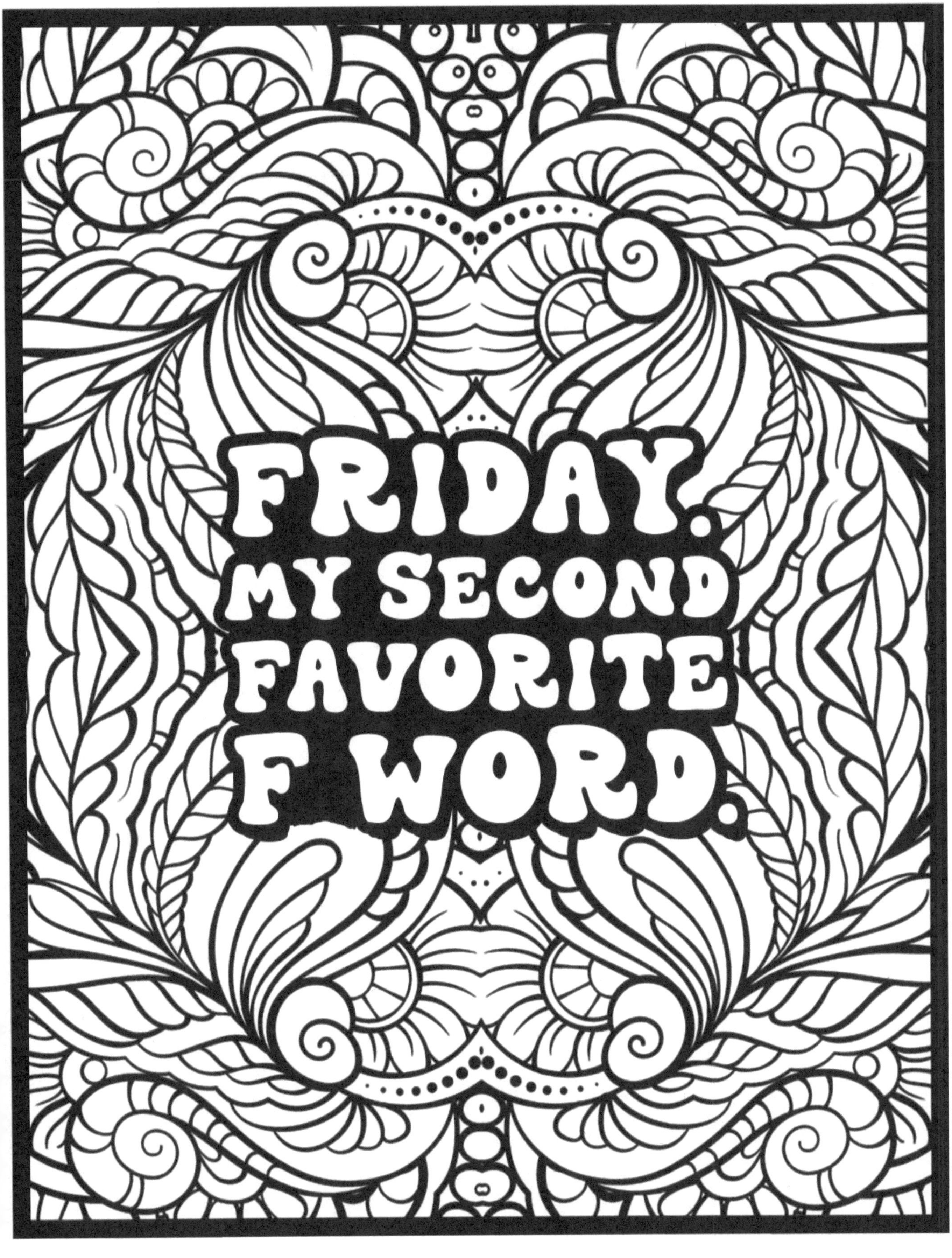
FRIDAY.
MY SECOND
FAVORITE
F WORD.

I SUFFER FROM
RESTING
NURSING
STUDENT
FACE

I CAN'T FIX
STUPID
BUT I CAN FIX
WHAT STUPID
DOES

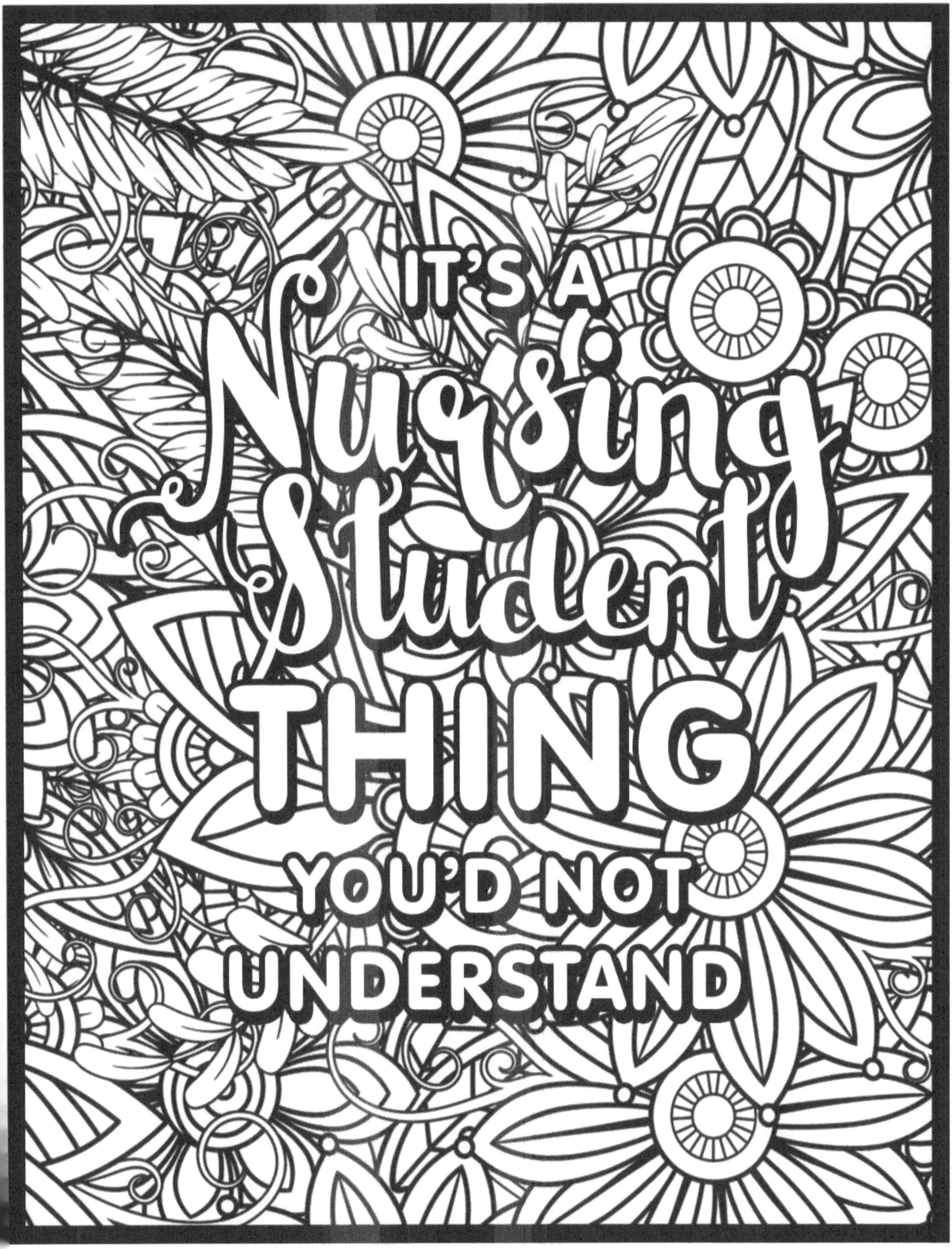
IT'S A
Nursing
Student
THING
YOU'D NOT
UNDERSTAND

Made in United States
Troutdale, OR
12/12/2024

26355241R00024